Fun With Jewish Holiday Rhymes

by Sylvia Rouss

Illustrated by Lisa Steinberg

UAHC Press · New York, New York

To my family,
Jeff, Gabrielle, Shannan, and Jordan

Sylvia A. Rouss

To Sol

Lisa Steinberg

Library of Congress Cataloging-in-Publication Data
Rouss, Sylvia A.
    Fun with Jewish holiday rhymes / by Sylvia A. Rouss;
illustrated by Lisa Steinberg.
        p.   cm.
    Summary: Illustrated rhymes accompanied by movement
activities introduce the holidays of the Jewish calendar.
    ISBN 0-8074-0463-2 (alk. paper) : $10.95
    1. Fasts and feasts—Judaism—Juvenile poetry.   2. Jewish
religious poetry, American.   3. Children's poetry, American.
[1. Fasts and feasts—Judaism—Poetry.   2. American
poetry.]   I. Steinberg, Lisa, ill. II. Title.
PS3568.08885F86   1992
296.4'3—dc20
91-40931
CIP
AC

The rhyme "This Old Lady" is adapted from the story "The Fat
Old Lady" from the book *Super Story Telling* by Elaine Catron
and Barbara Parks. Published by T.S. Denison, Minneapolis,
Minnesota 55431. With their permission.

This book is printed on acid-free paper
Copyright © 1992 by
The UAHC Press
Manufactured in the United States of America
10 9 8 7 6 5 4 3 2 1

Contents

Introduction

As a teacher of young children, I have noticed how much they enjoy rhymes and movement activities. Add the joy of Jewish celebration and the result is a fun-filled introduction to the holiday cycle.

In addition to building language skills and teaching Judaic symbols and concepts, the book also will help children learn to count, to add, and to subtract.

Most importantly, these rhymes motivate children to learn with a smile.

I hope parents, grandparents, siblings, and teachers, too, will enjoy reciting these verses with the little ones.

Rosh Hashanah

Five Little Shofars

Five little shofars in a row. *(Count on fingers)*

The first one said, "I'm hard to blow."
The second one said, "My sound is low."
The third one said, "I'm the best you know."
The fourth one said, "That's really not so."
The fifth one said, "I've got to go."

Five little shofars in a row.
Five little shofars blow, blow, blow.

The Shofar's Sound

The shofar's sound is loud and clear.
It has a sound I love to hear.
A sound that says, "Happy New Year."

Rosh Hashanah

Rosh Hashanah will soon be here.
It's the beginning of the year.

We go to temple and listen to the shofar's sound.
We eat a special challah—its shape is round.

We eat apples dipped in honey sweet.
They taste so good! Oh, what a treat!

We send Leshanah Tovah cards to our friends.
Before we know it the holiday ends.

1

The Little Shofar

I have a little shofar.
It makes a lovely sound.
I blow it for the new year,
When it comes around.

Rosh Hashanah Is Here

Rosh Hashanah is here at last.
Sound the shofar. Give a blast!
Leshanah Tovah is the way
To say "Happy New Year" on this day.

Five Little Apples

Five little apples, not any more. *(Count on fingers)*
I give one to _____ *(child's name)*,
And now there are four.
Four little apples are what I see.
I give one to _____,
And now there are three.
Three little apples for me and you.
I give one to _____,
And now there are two.
Two little apples; oh, what fun!
I give one to _____,
And now there is one.
One little apple, only one.
I give one to _____,
And now there are none.

Yom Kippur

Jonah

Jonah took a little sail
And found himself inside a whale.
He said, "It's very clear to me.
This is not the place to be.
Listen, God, help me, please.
Make this whale take a sneeze."
Aaaaaaaaachoo!

Yom Kippur

Yom Kippur is here at last.
It's a holiday on which we fast.
We go to temple and spend the day.
We ask for forgiveness when we pray.

3

Sukot

I Built A Little Sukah

(Tune: "I Made a Little Dreidel")

I built a little sukah.
I built it out of wood.
I hammered it together,
Just as I knew I could.

Refrain:
Oh, sukah, sukah, sukah,
I built it out of wood.
I hammered it together,
Just as I knew I could.

On top I placed some branches,
So I could see the sky.
Inside I hung some apples.
I hung them up so high. (*Repeat refrain*)

Inside I waved the lulav
And the etrog, too.
Inside I placed a table
With two chairs for me and you. (*Repeat refrain*)

Let's eat our dinner in it.
I know it will be fun.
Come, join us if you want to.
Come, join us everyone. (*Repeat refrain*)

Five Little Fruits

Five little fruits want to sway
From our sukah beam today.

The orange said, "I have a good taste.
Tie a string around my waist."
"I'm delicious," said the plum.
"Tie a string around my 'tummy-tum.'"
The apple said, "I'm very little.
Tie a string around my middle."
The banana said, "How will it feel?
Tie a string around my peel."
The grapes said, "Please, don't let us drop.
Tie a string around the top."

"Hang us in the sukah, oh, so high.
Let us watch the clouds go by."

So Many Fruits

There are so many fruits for you and me.
What kind of fruit does _____(child's name) see?

Build A Sukah, 1,2,3

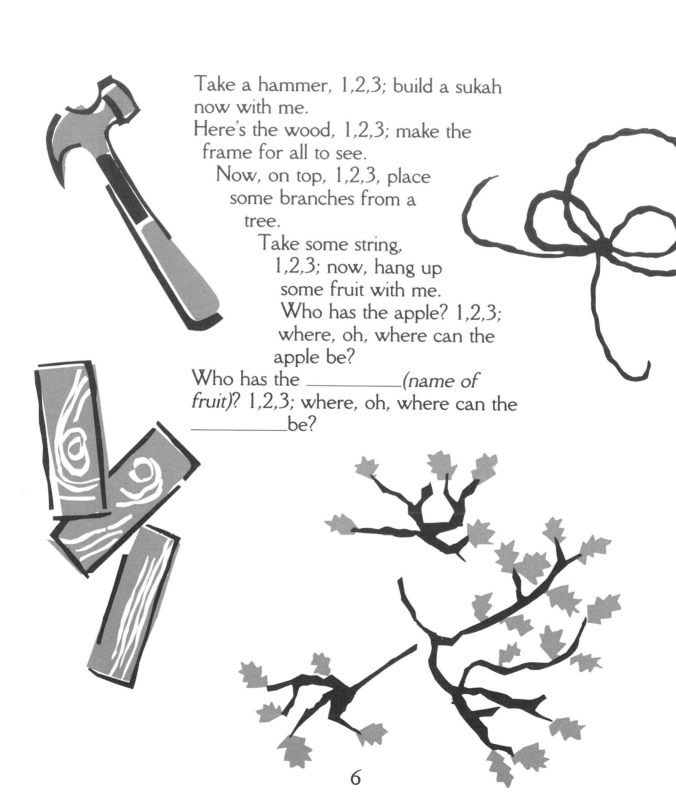

Take a hammer, 1,2,3; build a sukah now with me.
Here's the wood, 1,2,3; make the frame for all to see.
Now, on top, 1,2,3, place some branches from a tree.
Take some string, 1,2,3; now, hang up some fruit with me.
Who has the apple? 1,2,3; where, oh, where can the apple be?
Who has the _____(name of fruit)? 1,2,3; where, oh, where can the _____be?

Simchat Torah

Simchat Torah

Lift the Torah way up high. *(Raise hands)*
You can do it if you try.
Wave your flag all around. *(Wave hands)*
Do not let it touch the ground.
March around the synagogue now. *(Stamp feet)*
March with me, I'll show you how. *(March)*

Torah

Torah teaches us the way
We should live our lives each day.
We love the Torah; yes, we do.
It's a book for every Jew.

Chanukah

Five Strong Maccabees

One little Maccabee knows what to do. *(Count on fingers)*
Along comes another, and now there are two.
Two little Maccabees want to be free.
Along comes another, and now there are three.
Three little Maccabees go off to war.
Along comes another, and now there are four.
Four little Maccabees see one more arrive.
He marches with them, and now there are five.

Five strong Maccabees go off to war.
It's Judah Maccabee and his brothers four.
They fought Antiochus who was so bad.
They won the war and the Jews were glad.

Five Spinning Dreidels

Five little dreidels spinning all around. *(Count on fingers)*

The first one said, "I'll never touch the ground."
The second one said, "I'll spin all day."
The third one said, "I'll spin away."
The fourth one said, "I'll never stop."
The fifth one said, "I'll never drop."

Five little dreidels spin so fast.
Five little dreidels fall at last.

Five Little Dreidels

One little dreidel, shiny and new. *(Count on fingers)*
Finds another, and that makes two.
Two little dreidels spin as fast as can be.
They find another, and that makes three.
Three little dreidels look for one more.
They find another, and that makes four.
Four little dreidels see another arrive.
They all spin together, and that makes five.

Spin, Little Dreidels

Spin, little dreidels, go, go, go. *(Turn)*
Spin, little dreidels, now, go slow. *(Turn slowly)*
Spin, little dreidels, jump so high. *(Jump)*
Spin, little dreidels, reach for the sky. *(Stretch arms upward)*
Spin, little dreidels, touch your nose. *(Touch nose)*
Spin, little dreidels, stand on your toes. *(Stand on toes)*
Spin, little dreidels, take a hop. *(Hop on one foot)*
Spin, little dreidels, don't you stop. *(Keep hopping)*
Spin, little dreidels, spin around. *(Turn)*
Spin, little dreidels, drop to the ground. *(Sit)*

On Chanukah

On Chanukah we eat latkes baked in oil. *(Rub tummy)*

We eat chocolate gelt wrapped in gold foil. *(Pretend to unwrap gelt)*

We spin the dreidel with delight. *(Twirl fingers)*

We light the menorah—what a beautiful sight! *(Hold up eight fingers)*

Five Little Pieces Of Chanukah Gelt

I have five little pieces of Chanukah gelt. *(Count on fingers)*

The first one said, "Eat me up before I melt."
The second one said, "I have gold foil on both my sides."

The third one said, "Peel it to see where the chocolate hides."
The fourth one said, "Eat me up fast."
The fifth one said, "I am the last."

Chanukah gelt is so good to eat.
Chanukah gelt is my favorite treat.

Nine Little Candles

Nine little candles—what a sight!
They stand in the menorah and look so bright.

This one said, "I want to sway."
This one said, "I'm melting away."
This one said, "I'm still pretty tall."
This one said, "I'm getting small."
This one said, "I feel like skipping."
This one said, "My wax is dripping."
This one said, "I have no more light."
This one said, "It's the last Chanukah night."

The shamash said with a shout,
"I'll be the last candle to go out!"

"For eight long days, we did burn.
We'll see you next Chanukah when we return."

So Many Candles

There are so many candles,
Standing straight and tall.
Help me count them.
Let's count them all.
1,2,3,4,5,6,7,8.
You're doing fine.
Count the shamash.
That makes nine.

Five Little Latkes

Five little latkes, not any more. *(Count on fingers)*
I'll give one to _____ *(child's name)*,
And now there are four.
Four little latkes are what I see.
I'll give one to _____,
And now there are three.
Three little latkes for me and you.
I'll give one to _____,
And now there are two.
Two little latkes—oh, what fun!
I'll give one to _____,
And now there is one.
One little latke, only one.
I'll give it to _____,
And now there are none.

I Like Latkes

I like latkes.
Yes, I do!
I like latkes.
How about you?

I like latkes.
_____ *(child's name)* does,
too.
We like latkes.
How about you?

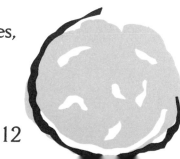

Yummy Latkes

I like to eat a latke. *(Pretend to eat)*
It tastes so good and yummy. *(Lick lips)*
I top it with some applesauce *(Cup left hand*
and place on right)
And put it in my tummy. *(Rub tummy)*

Five Little Latkes In The Frying Pan

Five little latkes in the frying pan. *(Count on fingers)*
I'd like to eat them if I can.

The first one said, "I'm frying in oil."
The second one said, "I've been placed on foil."
The third one said, "I'm very good to eat."
The fourth one said, "I'm a Chanukah treat."
The fifth one said, "I know you'll like me.
Take a bite, and you will see."

Tu Bishvat

Five Little Trees

This little tree has lots of wood.
This little tree has fruit so good.
This little tree, see how straight it grows.
This little tree bends when the wind blows.
This little tree is here to say,
"I'm glad it's Tu Bishvat today!"

Five Little Trees In A Row

Five little trees standing in a row. *(Count on fingers)*
Five little trees swaying to and fro.

The first one said, "My figs are good to eat."
The second one said, "My almonds are a treat."
The third one said, "Come, sit in my shade."
The fourth one said, "Climb on up. Don't be afraid!"
The fifth one said, "It's Tu Bishvat you know."

Sing "Happy Birthday" to five little trees in a row.

14

One Little Tree

One little tree swaying in the breeze.
A second one said, "May I join you, please?"
The little tree said, "Yes, you may.
It is Tu Bishvat today."

Two little trees swaying in the breeze.
A third one said, "May I join you, please?"
The little trees said, "Yes, you may.
It is Tu Bishvat today."

How many trees sway in the breeze?
Count them now. Count them, please.
Three little trees sing as they sway,
"It is Tu Bishvat today."

Purim

Shushan Town

This is King Ahasuerus of Shushan Town.
He is the king; he wears a crown.
This is Queen Vashti with a frown.
She had to leave old Shushan Town.
Esther, a Jewish girl, became the new queen.
She was the prettiest girl the king had ever seen.
This is Mordechai, a brave and loyal Jew.
He's Esther's cousin and the king's friend, too.

This is Haman, a really mean guy.
He made the Jewish people cry.
But Queen Esther was so very brave.
The Jewish people she did save.

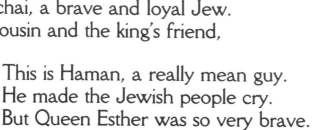

Packing For Shushan

I'm on my way to Shushan Town.
In my trunk I'll pack my crown.
I won't be needing any toys.
But I'll take my grogger to make some noise.
My Purim music I will bring
So you and I can dance and sing.

I'll take my Megillah; yes, indeed!
So the Purim story we can read.
"What else am I taking?" you may ask.
I can't forget my Purim mask.
Oops! I hope there's still some room.
I need to pack my Purim costume.
I might need something for my tummy.
I'll take my hamantashen; they're so yummy.
I'll take my shalach manot basket, too,
Filled with hamantashen for you and you.

16

Five Little Hamantashen

Five little hamantashen in a bakery shop. *(Count on fingers)*
All with yummy fillings showing through the top.
Along comes _____ *(child's name)* with a penny to pay.
_____takes a hamantash and runs far away.
(Repeat verse, counting down to one hamantash)

I'm A Little Grogger

(Tune: "I'm a Little Teapot")

I'm a little grogger; shake me around.
Here is my handle; now listen to my sound.
When I hear Haman's name, I shout.
Hold me tightly and wave me about.

Five Little Groggers

Five little groggers shake, shake, shake. *(Count on fingers)*

The first one said, "Hear the noise I make."
The second one said, "Hold me tightly; don't let go."
The third one said, "Shake me quickly; don't be slow."
The fourth one said. "Wave me all around."
The fifth one said, "I make a loud sound."

Five little groggers make so much noise.
Five little groggers are fun for girls and boys.

The Megillah

I'm a Megillah; look at me.
I'm a scroll as you can see.
I'm the one that you will need
When the Purim story you will read.

Passover
The story of Passover

The Jews of Egypt long ago
Had to work for the Pharaoh.
They had to work so hard all day
There wasn't any time to play.

One Jewish mommy said, "This isn't right.
We shouldn't work both day and night.
I do not want my son a slave.
My little boy, I'll try to save."

She set her baby boy afloat
In a little basket boat.
He was found by Pharaoh's daughter
When she came down to the water.

"I think I'll take this baby home.
I'll raise him as my very own.
The name Moses to him I'll give.
He will come with me to live."

When Moses grew up big and strong,
He said to Pharaoh, "What you do is wrong.
Let my people go today,
Or you will have a price to pay."

Pharaoh would not listen then;
So God sent plagues that numbered ten.
At last Pharaoh said, "You may have your way.
Moses, take your people and leave today."

The Jewish people, wanting bread,
With so little time, baked matzah instead.
They hurried across the parted sea.
The Jewish people at last were free.

Five Little Frogs

Five little frogs went out one night
And gave the Pharaoh quite a fright.
(Count on fingers)

The first one said, "I'll jump on his bed."
The second one said, "I'll jump on his head."
The third one said, "I'll jump on his toes."
The fourth one said, "I'll jump on his nose."
The fifth one said, "I'll jump on his face,
And then we can jump all over the place."

Five Little Birds

Five little birds sitting in the sun.
(Count on fingers)

The first one said, "Pesach is fun."
The second one said, "We can't eat any bread."
The third one said, "We'll eat matzah instead."
The fourth one said, "We'll get a little fatter."
The fifth one said, "That doesn't matter!"

The sun is going down; it's getting later.
Five little birds fly off to the seder.

19

Five Little Matzah Balls

Five little matzah balls jump into a pot.
   (Count on fingers)

The first one said, "I'm very hot."
The second one said, "I'm light as air."
The third one said, "I really don't care."
The fourth one said, "I'm nice and round."
The fifth one said, "I must weigh a pound."

Five little matzah balls
In my soup they go.
I will gladly eat them up.
I love Pesach so!

Making Matzah Balls

Let's put some matzah balls in the pot.
We've boiled the water. It is hot.

One matzah ball goes plop.
Two matzah balls go plop, plop.
Three matzah balls go plop, plop, plop.

My Haggadah

Here is my haggadah.
It helps me know
The story of Pesach
That happened long ago.

Five Little Matzot

I have five little matzot, not any more.
  (Count on fingers)
I give one to _____ *(child's name)*,
And now there are four.
Four little matzot are all I see.
I give one to _____,
And now there are three.
Three little matzot for me and you.
I give one to _____,
And now there are two.
Two little matzot—oh, what fun!
I give one to _____,
And now there is one.
One little matzah, only one.
I give it to _____,
And now there are none.

My Seder Plate

Here is a seder plate.
It looks brand new.
It holds five special symbols,
Which I now show to you.

The Afikoman

I'm looking for the afikoman.
I know that it's somewhere.
I've looked in every corner,
But it isn't anywhere.

I cannot find the afikoman.
It was hidden in my house.
Do you suppose that it was eaten
By a little mouse?

I found the afikoman.
I will tell you where.
It was where I never looked.
It was underneath my chair.

I took the afikoman.
I held it in my hand.
I ate it up for dessert.
I know you'll understand.

Elijah's Cup

Here I have Elijah's cup.
I fill it to the brim.
I hope he comes to drink it up,
And I'll catch a glimpse of him.

This Old Lady

This old lady loves to eat.
Passover foods are her favorite treat.

At one o'clock, she ate fried matzah in a dish.
At two o'clock, she had a piece of gefilte fish.
At three o'clock, she ate cream cheese and lox.
At four o'clock, she had matzah from a box.
At five o'clock, she ate brisket from a pot.
At six o'clock, she had matzah ball soup—steaming hot.
At seven o'clock, she ate a large piece of veal.
At eight o'clock, she had pancakes made from matzah meal.
At nine o'clock, she ate a Pesach candy bar.
At ten o'clock, she had macaroons from a jar.
At eleven o'clock, she ate Passover sponge cake.
At twelve o'clock, she had a stomachache.

Lag Ba'omer

Lag Ba'omer

Lag Ba'omer is such fun.
We'll have a picnic in the sun.
Come along, come with me.
Let us sit beneath this tree.

Lag Ba'omer Picnic

We're going on a Lag Ba'omer picnic.
What shall we pack?
We'll take along some _____ *(children's suggestions)*
And put them in our sack.

Shavuot

Here are the Ten Commandments as you can see.
They are for you, and they are for me.
God gave us the Ten Commandments on Shavuot day.
They are God's laws, which we all must obey.

The Ten Commandments

Here are the commandments.
There are ten as you can see.
Listen as I count them.
Count along with me.

Shabbat

Shabbat Time

Soon Shabbat will be here.
A holiday we hold so dear.
Help me set the table now.
Come along, I'll show you how.
The candles have a special place.
On our tablecloth of lace.
Here I place the Kiddush cup.
I take some wine and fill it up.
The challah I shall place right here.
The time for Shabbat is so near.

Shabbat Night

On this lovely Shabbat night,
The candles are a pretty sight. *(Hold up two fingers)*
The Kiddush cup I hold is mine. *(Cup hand)*
I take a little sip of wine. *(Pretend to take sip)*
I smell the challah with delight. *(Pretend to smell challah)*
I break a piece and take a bite. *(Pretend to eat)*